Successful Self-talk

A short guide on how to talk yourself into
the successful life you desire.

Copyright © 2023 by J.B. Waters
All rights reserved.
No portion of this book may be reproduced in any form
without written permission from the publisher or author,
except for the use of brief quotations in a book review.

Printed in the United States of America
Cover Design: J.B. Waters
Cover Image: Icon made by Three Musketeers from www.flaticon.com

First Printing, 2024

Published by 1888 House LLC

ISBN 978-1-7373645-4-2

Successful Self-talk

A short guide on how to talk yourself into
the successful life you desire.

J.B. Waters

Contents

Preface

v

Introduction

viii

Purpose Is the Prize

1

Time to Talk

6

Self-talk Types

31

Take Out the Trash

38

Truth or Trash

51

Word/Phrase Swap

56

Success Starts with Speech.
(Conclusion)

58

PREFACE

Since being a baby and you saying your first words the ability to speak has always seemed like magic. Whether those first words were no because that's what you heard the most, or "mama" or "dada" because that was the easiest to pronounce. Our words have always given us the power to manifest something into our physical world through their usage. As a baby, I'm sure you noticed that when you said "juice", juice appeared to you by way of your guardian or whoever was taking care of you. It seemed that your mere words could cause a reaction that led to you possessing anything you asked for. As an infant, words like please and thank you didn't matter as much. It was as if people were happy enough to hear you speak.

Somewhere in life, it got more complicated, and manners became more important to your dialogue. But even still with the addition of manners words didn't lose their manifesting powers. If anything, adding them to your dialogue granted you even more of what your heart desired. Yes, words have always been there to aid us even as babies. If words have been our greatest ally since childhood, when did they become our most feared enemy? At what point in life did the words we say out loud, become the words we say in our minds, and eventually the words we became slaves to? Children learn as much and as fast as you allow them to. Place a child in a world with stimulating experiences and watch how their mind engages and interacts. On the flipside place a child in an environment with less stimulating activities and the child is left only with its thoughts.

What do you believe would be the most dominant thoughts of a child left in isolation? What do you believe would be the most dominant thoughts of a child surrounded by stimulating and creative experiences? Is the way we speak to ourselves a reflection of what we hear around us? Does our self-talk originate from how people talk to us? What about a baby's first words, are the first words spoken just a reflection of its first words heard? Are the baby's inner thoughts already predetermined or does the baby have preexisting thoughts that go beyond genetics and epigenetics? In this guide, we will learn how self-talk can be determined by one's environment while also revealing the secret of enhancing the manifesting powers that words have. Words can build destroy, condemn, or liberate.

How we use these words to speak to ourselves can lead us to success or turmoil. In this guide, you will take a deep look at your everyday self-talk while noticing how your environment affects your life's narrative. Imagine a world without hearing, a world without speaking. Allow yourself to be open to the lessons provided in this guide, to help give you more insight on how you speak your external world into existence through your inner thoughts and speech.

Most of the talk we have with ourselves plays a greater role in the world we live in than the conversation we have with the world. I hope to become a pathway for you on this journey of learning proper words and emotions to project within to help lead you to the successful life you desire.

By the end of this guide, you will have more control over what you say and how you say it. You will truly master how to talk yourself into success instead of talking yourself into shame, sadness, and failure.

Introduction

As the final minutes of the test end, you begin to review your answers with a slight uncertainty. Spending several hours studying while everyone else went out on the weekend, felt like a sure-fire way to fly through the test. But it felt like you didn't study at all for some reason. As the hands on the clock seem to move super-fast, you begin to sweat uncontrollably. You look around at your classmates and notice most people are already done with the test. With an overwhelming amount of nervousness, you begin to think of what would happen if you failed this test.

All the doubt that compelled you to study starts to kick in and you begin to talk to yourself. *What if this test keeps me from moving on? How dumb do you have to be to study as hard as I did and still get nervous? Man, I'm the worst. Why did this stupid teacher make this test so long?* As you proceed to go through all the self-doubting dialogue in your head, you look up and realize that even more time has passed. Being unaware of the time, due to your distractive self-talk, you start to spiral out of control into more intense negative self-talk. *How is this stupid clock moving so fast? If only I woke up earlier, I could have studied some more. If only I had taken that practice exam one more time, I'm sure I would have known these last questions. Noticing you sweat anxiously the professor gives you some relief by asking if you're okay.* Not wanting to seem as if everything is falling apart, you quickly reply to the professor with confidence, "Yep, almost done, wrapping a few things up." The professor replies with a smile, "Great, sounds good." You suddenly realize that you weren't helping yourself at all by not being honest with the professor, so you decide to call it quits and complete the test to the best of your ability. At that moment, you feel it's best to finally let go and surrender to whatever the results of the test may be.

As you're finishing up the last few questions on the test, you start to feel more relieved by the fact that you are no longer worried. It was as if not overthinking and caring too much made all the answers appear. With the final questions being answered you start to think to yourself. *I do remember this. This is like the questions I answered last night before falling asleep.* The more you spoke to yourself the less anxious you felt. The timer went off as you filled in the last answer. Now that the test is over you feel even more relieved because you allowed yourself to be okay with not trying to control the outcome.

The professor decided to grade everyone's test on the spot since the test wasn't long. You begin to look around and notice how all the students who finished before you are looking as nervous as you were previously during the test. It was as if you had swapped places with them. As the professor passes the graded tests around, you hear students speaking out loud to themselves. Shouting angrily their disappointment with their test results. One after the other. "This is an outrage." "70, how is this possible?" "I breezed through these answers."

"80, this must be a mistake." The more tests the professor passes around, the more negative comments you hear from your classmates. The professor finally gets to your desk, and as the professor places the test on the table, he smiles and gives you a confident response, "Hey there, great job, I don't know if it was the sweating or the relaxing, but great work." You flip the paper over to your surprise you see in big red letters, 90. You only missed one question, which happened to be the first one.

This simple story of how our thoughts and the things we tell ourselves have a huge effect on how feelings reveal everything isn't how your mind perceives it to be. In this story, the student kept falling victim to negative self-talk which in turn made what was going on in the external world seem even worse.

This is the perfect example of how the way we talk to ourselves can either enslave us or set us free. Think about the last time you were feeling frustrated or confused. Once you have this memory locked into your head, I want you to recall how you were talking to yourself during those moments. Can you remember if you were talking negatively before you had those feelings or were you feeling those emotions before you were talking to yourself? Most of the time when we have feelings that are strongly felt whether that be positive or negative, we will have some mental dialogue to go along with it. A lot of self-talk is actually because of how we feel externally, but the majority of what happens externally is caused by something that happens internally.

      The purpose of this short guide is to teach you how to manifest and summon the external world you desire through the internal conversation you have with yourself on a daily. This guide was created to let you the reader see a realistic view of when, what, and how you talk to yourself negatively. The goal is to show you how to identify what you're currently saying so you can replace it with mindful self-talk that leads to success. Yes, successful self-talk.

Chapter 1

Purpose Is the Prize

I believe the universe has endowed every creature with the innate desire to fulfill a purpose. Every creature is genetically hardwired to serve some purpose in its lifetime. From birds soaring the skies in search of shelter or food to humans creating tools with our bare hands for protection, every creature is driven by purpose. The most powerful concept and difference we have as human beings is our purpose is derived from free will.

Our ability to tell our minds something and watch our physical bodies carry the thought out is one of the greatest things that separates us from other species on this planet. Humans are not bound by the instincts that our genetic code carries like other species. We have the choice of free will, thought, and action to live our lives the way we see fit as individuals. That thought alone makes you realize or at least question if the mind is stronger than the vessel that carries it. But as they say with great power comes great responsibility. I'm no professor or academic scholar but I truly feel the concept of "free will" purpose is our superpower and can be our kryptonite if not embraced mindfully. This is the part that we as humans have lost sight of, we forget how powerful our minds are and the role it plays in our overall gift of purpose. In this chapter of the guide, we will discuss how the goals and purpose we place on ourselves affect the type of self-talk we have as individuals. This chapter will allow you to see how everyone's self-talk is relative to the standards that they have for themselves.

I've noticed in my life when I have a certain goal in mind, my mind has already had a conversation with itself about what the results should somewhat look like, it's as if my mind's eyes see the result before my physical eyes do. In my opinion, this can be a good or bad thing for several reasons. I will address my reasoning in two ways, first I will discuss the positive view of this type of thinking and how it relates to self-talk and then I will discuss the negative view of thinking and how it relates to self-talk.

This thinking can be viewed as positive if used as a form of creativity, structure, or planning. Every human-made object we see starts as an idea inside someone's mind before it becomes tangible for all the world to see. Each person had to have an initial vision of what they were trying to create or accomplish. Essentially each person plants a seed within their minds that can grow into whatever it is they were trying to bring to life. Everything that we believe gives us purpose begins its journey in our minds. This too is another gift from God, source, and the universe to show us how different we are as humans. Our ability to have a vision in our minds that can drive us to make that vision a reality is what makes us unique from all other species. The fluidity of these visions and how they are not hardwired in our instincts gives us this Godlike power.

Now on the flip side, the gift of our mind's eye can lead us to frustration, confusion, and disappointment, by overanalyzing the result of what we think should happen. Our minds are so powerful that we can place ourselves in an emotional state that can be triggered by the idea of a physical event or object without possessing or carrying out the event in real-time. Once we begin to convince our minds of a certain truth, that truth starts to become our reality in the physical realm or form. The power that we possess by overthinking a result without being in that present time can bring more harm to our present day than necessary.

It may seem like the positive side of being able to accomplish great feats can become obsolete if not used with the intent of making sure your thoughts don't get too ahead of your actions. Your self-talk can be seen as the coach of the mental game of life, guiding you in whatever direction you are trying to go. A coach doesn't have to be a positive force in your life. The coach is designed to reinforce any goal or effort that you already have set in place. When you have a certain view on how your plans and ideas should go, you talk to yourself in a manner that reinforces the certainty of that goal becoming accomplished.

If you are a very focus-oriented person then most of your talk will be centered around growth, progress, and effort. If you're more of a doubtful, insecure type of person then your internal dialogue may be more discouraging, dark, and pessimistic. Either way, your overall view on life will be the main metric you gauge your self-talk on. In a sense, you're confirming with yourself via your internal dialogue about the progress of your goals or ideas. The stress and worry that comes with making sure you meet the mental vision you fabricated in your mind may not be worth the effort if, in turn, it gives the opposite result. This essentially can be the biggest downside to envisioning your goals while trying to move towards them. Imagine how many times you've done self-analysis, telling your mind you either do better or this or that needs to happen, or you start to go down your mental checklist of how far or close you are to that goal. The purpose we place on ourselves in life plays a major role in how we view our progression and growth. Would you care as much about the things you tell yourself if the topic of discussion wasn't important to you? Even the smallest of tasks include some form of self-talk. Picture yourself in the kitchen cooking and trying a new recipe. Can you imagine right now all the different levels of internal dialogue you have at that moment?

Most of our deepest and darkest fears don't get externally expressed. If most of how we talk to ourselves doesn't come out for the rest of the world to hear then where does it go? This question is the premise of this guide. The negative talk that you don't release and manifest to the outside world takes a toll on the only option it has left which is you. That's why I'm a firm believer in positive self-talk, but if you can't master the art of successful talk, then it's very imperative to have someone to speak to or an external outlet to express your negative thoughts healthily.

Our purpose is seen as being a part of our destiny, and if we can't control how we view the progress within our purpose then we can't control our destiny. This guide is designed to help you control your destiny, by controlling your approach to finding and completing your purpose through successfully talking yourself into all you desire to become. Next time you begin to think about if you're meeting up to your self-imposed standards towards your goals and purpose remember to reinforce your mind with a dialogue that serves your whole being best. Humans weren't born with only a mouth and mind. But these two parts of our beings have so much power over the rest.

Chapter 2
Time to Talk

For the sake of this guide let's just say you live in a city or a place where the weather changes three times every two to four hours. All jokes aside, this place could be Atlanta. My hometown seems to have some of the most unpredictable weather I've ever seen. You would truly have to see it to believe it. But anyway, I could write a whole book about the weather in Atlanta. Imagine you're leaving your house around midday and it's pouring down outside like those super big raindrops, the "cats and dogs" kind. Do you think this would be a moment in which you have some form of self-talk, that would be relative to the event at hand? Could you picture what type of self-talk you would have? Would you be in a state of frustration, depression, or maybe surprise? The current weather would have you thinking and talking to yourself about the condition. Let's say you drive 10 minutes to your destination and upon arrival the weather changes to where there isn't a cloud in sight and it's 100 degrees suddenly. Now what kind of dialogue would you have with these conditions? Would this sudden change in weather change the narrative of your internal dialogue? Would your dialogue be consistent with the dialogue you had while it was raining when you first left your house? Could you picture yourself trying to make sense of the situation at hand? When you head back home from your destination clouds begin to cover the sky and large snowflakes rapidly fall from the sky. So much snow is falling that it starts to impair your vision to drive, so you drive slow enough to the point where your car is barely moving.

With all three weather conditions happening in such a short period, I'm sure your mind doesn't know what to think. No matter how much reasoning you could try to come up with there wouldn't be any sensible explanation that could keep you from trying to comprehend these events. Without a doubt, this event would cause you to have all types of internal dialogue. The dialogue would come with some emotion, whether that be anger, frustration, or disappointment. Although this is a very extreme situation that is pretty much impossible to occur. We experience moments in our lives that cause us to react to them with some form of self-talk. Some of these moments are large significant eventful times in our lives or very small moments in our lives. No matter the magnitude our self-talk can always be connected to an event or moment in time that causes it. In this chapter, we will identify and write down the times we most frequently talk to ourselves and the reason we are having these conversations. This chapter is designed to help you become more aware of the events that trigger your self-talk and how to control the dialogue to the point that it's no longer a reflection of the things that trigger negative self-talk in your life.

Triggers & Times

This section of the guide is for you to look at all the possible triggers and times that may cause you to have conscious self-talk. By conscious self-talk, I mean self-talk that you are consciously aware of due to an action that caused it. This is also self-talk that you are actively controlling and doing with the intent of accomplishing an outcome or goal.

In my quest to find and identify the triggers we commonly share, I looked at the four most prevalent factors that I found in myself and my peers. These are the triggers that I identified among most of my peers and myself. I call them "4 Trigger Pillars". These pillars are the basis of the factors that trigger some form of self-talk/ dialogue whether that be negative or positive in a person. Each pillar represents the foundation from which any of your self-talk is connected or derived. The pillars are mutually exclusive to each person at different times but can also be interconnected depending on the situation that is causing the self-talk.

Each pillar can be solely related to the choices you make or don't make. Some can be completely related to externals.
I will use this section of the chapter to explain in detail the basis and ideology behind each pillar and how it relates to our self-talk.

4 TRIGGER PILLARS:
Emotional
Perspective
Environment
Goal/Purpose

Pillar I- Emotional

Emotional triggers cause a certain self-talk due to how you're feeling in that moment. Most people's self-talk is relative to their emotional state. For instance, when most people are feeling angry, their self-talk may include curse words or offensive language. These words may be aimed towards oneself or towards the person who helps draw that emotion out of them. Interconnection comes into play when an external source causes an emotion that leads to a certain type of self-talk whether that be negative or positive. Our emotions are energy in its rawest form within the human heart and mind. Why is it so important to be aware of your external or internal dialogue when you are in a heightened emotional state? We must identify the answer to this question to truly understand how our emotions play into the words we tell ourselves.

Below you will see places for you to write down your most common emotions and the internal dialogue that goes with them

Emotion-

Time-

Self-talk-

Emotion-

Time-

Self-talk-

Emotion-

Time-

Self-talk-

Emotion-

Time-

Self-talk-

Emotion-

Time-

Self-talk-

Emotion-

Time-

Self-talk-

Emotion-

Time-

Self-talk-

Emotion-

Time-

Self-talk-

Emotion-

Time-

Self-talk-

Emotion-

Time-

Self-talk-

Once you identify all the emotions that trigger your self-talk, you will be able to control the self-talk no matter what emotion is associated with it. If denial is the first step in not growing, acceptance and identification are the first steps. There are several moments in life where we find ourselves having self-talk that is a direct reflection of how we're feeling in that moment. The most powerful but somewhat detrimental fact is that sometimes, our feelings about a situation or event may not be 100% accurate. This leads us to inaccurate self-talk based on our feelings related to something. That's why it's imperative to understand why and how you're feeling.

We have certain self-talk based on our view of a situation. Perhaps if someone else was in the same situation they would have a different perspective that gives them a different emotional outcome that ends in a different self-talk.

Pillar II– Perspective

The way we view life and the situations we face can have a great impact on our emotions, mental dialogue, and choices. Each person sees the world from a lens that is based on their personal experiences, upbringing, and ideologies. When we reflect on a certain topic, situation, or option, we naturally revert to our mind's memories to help decide whether this or that thing is true, important, or real to us. Our perspective plays a major role in the type of dialogue we have, while also giving us a clue on exactly why we have that dialogue. Sometimes we find ourselves being judgmental or disagreeable about a topic based solely on our perspective about said topic.

The perspective pillar is designed for you to think about those situations that cause you to feel passionately opinionated. Can you think of a time when your outlook on a situation wasn't followed by some self-talk? If you're being completely honest with yourself, you'll most likely say no. The perspective pillar is meant to help you identify if your perspective is directly correlated with the self-talk you're having within a certain moment. For example, let's say you witness something that you don't agree with, and you know it goes against your moral compass. Do you instantly have judgmental self-talk that validates the moral standards in your mind, or do you first look at all sides of the situation and ask yourself how much you know about the situation to properly conduct that sort of self-talk? Perspective is the calibration we use when weighing our belief systems.

Two separate people may engage in the same difficult task but carry out the task with two different attitudes and get two different results due to their separate perspectives on life. They both have the same object to weigh but will have two different results because of the calibration of each scale they use in their lives. Our perspective is also based on the expectations we have in life. When we have an outlook on something, most of the time it's derived from the predetermined results we're looking to get.

For instance, if you're driving in bumper-to-bumper traffic that may cause you to be late to your destination, your perspective on that event may be negative due to your expectations. In that moment your expectation fed your perspective which in turn caused a specific type of self-talk related to the whole event or outcome. In this section I want you to think about one to five of the most important events that you have in a week. Then I want you to write down the most common perspective, outlook, and attitude you have on those events. Lastly, I want you to write down the type of self-talk associated with those events.

For example, my event is my weekly gym session. My perspective is some days, I don't know if I should go, due to me not eating enough calories. Some days, my self-talk is negative and may consist of thoughts like *If I could eat as much food as I want then I could work out with no hesitation.* Some days my self-talk is positive like *it's all good. I'll just work out a little for the sake of discipline and muscle memory.* This exercise allows you to see your self-talk while helping you evaluate if this is the type of dialogue you truly feel or if it's caused by your emotions or perspective about the situation. Seeing the dialogue allows you to align your true intentions with the results of the dialogue you have with yourself that is related to any given situation or moment in your life.

Below you will see places for you to write down the most common events, your perspective on the events, and the type of self-talk that occurs during these events.

Event-

Perspective-

Self-talk-

Event-

Perspective-

Self-talk-

Event-

Perspective-

Self-talk-

Event-

Perspective-

Self-talk-

Event-

Perspective-

Self-talk-

Event-

Perspective-

Self-talk-

Event-

Perspective-

Self-talk-

Event-

Perspective-

Self-talk-

Event-

Perspective-

Self-talk-

Event-

Perspective-

Self-talk-

    Now that you have a clear visual on how perspective connects to your internal dialogue, you can control the type of self-talk related to it. The whole purpose of this guide is to use all your mental dialogue to help give you the ultimate life you desire, a life of success, prosperity, and peace. Our minds are like computer programs that can only run and operate on the information it's fed. Whatever you allow to enter your mind essentially creates the thoughts you have, which in turn creates the environment you live in. For most people, their environment controls their thoughts and self-talk. In this next pillar, we will discuss how our environment plays a major role in the self-talk we have and the emotions that come with it.

Pillar III- Environment

There's an old saying that goes "You're a product of your environment." and I believed that for a small amount of time growing up as a kid. I noticed most people in my neighborhood looked and had the same quality of life. Luckily God chose my mom early and as she grew in her faith in God our environment started to change. But I say that to say, for the first few years of my life my environment shaped my view on the world.

Even as a kid I always felt like I was different not to sound hyperbolic but by the age of six, I felt I had a grasp on the laws of the universe and how it relates to self-awareness. I became aware that my story was one story of billions of stories being told on this earth. I determined that I would be the author of my own story. Our environment influences our perspective and emotions when we're growing and finding ourselves. There are certain times throughout the day that you can find your self-talk being directly connected to the environment you're in. I decided to do a more modern exercise since we are in the age of artificial intelligence and supercomputers.

For this exercise I want you to do voice memos for 1 hour, 1 day, and 1 week on any time you feel your environment is causing you to have any form of self-talk, whether negative or positive. For all the negative self-talk write down what environment you were in and how you felt. (You may also write down what you felt as well). *For the sake of utilizing technology writing your dialogue down isn't required. I'm expressing this option for those who love to journal and write.* For all the positive dialogue, narrow down the difference between the environments that cause negative versus positive self-talk.

If you've noticed or read my previous vademecum "Have Your Happiness" then you know I love to focus on addressing and identifying the root cause of our feelings, actions, and thoughts. Most people are less self-aware than they know, and identifying your inner attributes gives you a road map to change while allowing you to have some form of accountability with your newfound enlightenment.

Negative Dialogue:

Environment-

Emotion-

Exact Dialogue-

Environment-

Emotion-

Exact Dialogue-

Environment-

Emotion-

Exact Dialogue-

Positive Dialogue:

Environment-

Emotion-

Difference-

Environment-

Emotion-

Difference-

Environment-

Emotion-

Difference-

    Now that you've identified and compared the exact negative and positive dialogue you've associated your environment with, you can now focus on reprogramming your mind to essentially have mind over matter. The pressures of life can be so daunting that we allow our environment to completely dictate our thoughts. The first part of this guide is the "what". This is where we find exactly what our self-talk is, what causes it, and how it operates daily.

    Throughout our day, we have moments of dialogue that are previews of our beliefs behind our emotions, perspective, and purpose. Our goals/purpose can be the driving force for our lives. We place so much weight on what we think we were born to do or be. People spend hours applying energy and effort toward this supposed purpose or goal. Imagine how many people live angry, lost, or frustrated lives due to not believing they are accomplishing their life purpose. The amount of negative self-talk that comes with the doubt associated with someone's life purpose drives some to the point of retreatment to no longer pursue their goals.

In the next pillar, we will discuss goals and purpose and how they set the tone for the type of self-talk we engage in daily. Goals can be very useful especially when someone understands how they can positively affect your life outside of their intrinsic value. We as humans set goals for many reasons. For some it may be for acquisition, for others, it may be for the sake of a contribution, but for most, it's the emotional and mental reinforcing it brings.

Our goals are closely set to our purpose because they are both related to the journey of life. In fact, neither is identified at birth and only comes into existence through time and effort. The next pillar will describe our initial thoughts and feelings toward accomplishing our goals and purpose.

Pillar IV- Goals/Purpose

In this section I want you to write down however many goals you have, whether that be short term or long term doesn't matter. This is totally up to you, but with each goal I want you to write the time frame you set to accomplish them, your initial emotion about accomplishing them and how you think you'll feel, and the type of self-talk you will have when you accomplish the goals.

Goal-

Deadline-

Initial Self-talk-

Actual Self-talk/Emotion Once Accomplished-

Goal-

Deadline-

Initial Self-talk-

Actual Self-talk/Emotion Once Accomplished-

Goal-

Deadline-

Initial Self-talk-

Actual Self-talk/Emotion Once Accomplished-

Goal-

Deadline-

Initial Self-talk-

Actual Self-talk/Emotion Once Accomplished-

Goal-

Deadline-

Initial Self-talk-

Actual Self-talk/Emotion Once Accomplish

      Life can be very unpredictable at times which can cause a lot of anxiety due to the uncertainty that comes with life. Most times people lose sleep over what they can't control. This can be a very unhealthy way to live.

The amount of negative self-talk that comes with uncontrollable situations is worse than dealing with the ones you can control. The difference is at least with the controllable you can alter your external situation and results by your internal dialogue. But no amount of self-talk can directly alter or change any situation that is out of your control.

Our goals are responsibilities that directly affect our lives and mostly rely on our efforts, but there will be times when other external factors affect the accomplishments of our goals. The external factors for some people are so powerful that they resort to negative self-talk. Writing down your goals as you did in the previous exercise will assist you with becoming more aware of how you're letting your goals positively or negatively affect you based on your self-talk.

This exercise was designed to assist you with becoming more accountable for how you react to controllable goals versus how you react to the uncontrollable factors that come along with your goals. The most powerful keys are self-awareness, reflection, and accountability. These three keys can help keep you in a positive headspace when faced with opposition during your journey to your goal. Being able to stay positive during difficult times isn't an easy feat. We all have moments where enough is enough and we just can't see the positive.

Why are some people more optimistic than others? Do you consider yourself more optimistic than your peers? In the next chapter, we will discuss the two types of self-talk.

Over the years I've managed to come up with two different types of self-talk through observing others and my battle with staying successful in my mental dialogue. It's amazing what you hear and learn by listening to internal dialogue.

Chapter 3
Self-talk Types

Throughout my entire life, I've always believed I was a person who could see the positive side of any situation. Some can attest that I've been the voice of reason in the past or the person that people confided in when they needed to hear the truth. Even though hearing the truth wasn't always positive, I figured people would rather hear it from me, since I enjoy the honesty that comes with my optimism.

I will not discuss any scientific facts to describe why I feel some people are more optimistic than others but instead, I will explain how I came about finding what I describe as the two types of self-talk. These concepts came about by way of my personal life experiences and observations. There were days in my past when I searched within to understand why my life was in the condition it was in. There were also days when I listened to people's stories to get more insight into why their lives were the way they were. Trial and error, pain, and suffering led me to the findings I'm discussing today.

As we discuss the two types of self-talk, I encourage everyone to take mental note of which one resonates with you and why. The purpose of this chapter is to learn how the types of self-talk are interconnected and how they both can be beneficial to your growth process.

Self-Talk Type 1

Successful Suffering Self-Talk

In life, I've noticed that most people try to work their issues out in their heads before verbally expressing them to the rest of the world. It's as If we believe people won't see who we truly are if we refrain from verbalizing our ideas, thoughts, and emotions. I've spent several years listening to people describe their deepest thoughts to me solely because I made myself available to listen.

People verbalize how painful life has been for them but the reward of not weighing the risk is tenfold in terms of what had to be endured to succeed. The people I've spoken to in past conversations suffered so much that it inspired them to grow. They ultimately convinced themselves that they would succeed in life by primarily focusing on what they tell their minds and their perspective about their journey. Our relationship with suffering determines how we view the world and situations.

Picture the last time you felt like something was causing you pain due to its difficulty level. How did you view the situation before realizing it was harmful or painful? Did your view of the situation change once your mind recognized and identified with the suffering that came along with it? In my experience, how someone reacts to pain and suffering will tell you a lot about how they react to life in general. Why is that? Do you think people who deal with suffering a lot easier than those who don't have some sort of secret? The answer is yes and no in my opinion. If you ask me the secret is being aware and utilizing the power of endurance. Endurance allows someone to stick with tough situations that can potentially benefit them in the long run, regardless of the initial pain or difficulty that comes with it.

The way we react to suffering gives us some form of overall perspective on life; good or bad. Our conditions and norms determine what we tolerate. What we consider ourselves to be is used to give us an idea of what we can handle in present and future moments. Many of you are probably thinking to be optimistic during tough times you must go through them, and you would be correct to assume so. We can't acquire endurance without having things to endure. The events we go through train our minds to adjust every time we go through them. There is a slight difference between learning through pain and learning through fear. I will discuss this in further detail in the coming paragraphs.

But to touch on it briefly, some people have fearful conversations with themselves to avoid pain or suffering which leads them to success. This may work for some in the short term, but it never addresses the root cause of the issue. The fear-based self-talk always comes back in another form that's less helpful than the endurance of suffering-based self-talk. The long-term positive effect suffering has on the mind can be looked at like this because the result will always outweigh the initial pain if embraced properly.

Once you identify the worst things that can happen and become fully aware and comfortable with that, you no longer live in fear of the possibility. Once you mentally, spiritually, and emotionally place yourself at rock bottom and realize what dwells there you can only see the upside to a situation. Suffering reveals this test to us all. This is the test of how we can choose to act or react towards any given situation or perspective in life.

I want you to think about someone successful in life you admire. Can you think of times when they made public speeches or interviews? Think about when they were asked to explain their story of success and how it came about. If you can remember, you will acknowledge that all these people put some emphasis and enthusiasm on how they had to suffer and remain positive throughout their journey. Every person you think of faces challenges that require them to use positive self-talk to keep them moving forward. The thoughts we have either contest or reinforce our beliefs about our goals.

The major thing to realize is that most self-talk comes from experiences you have daily. People who learn to have positive experiences with themselves no matter the situation typically have more positive self-talk/internal dialogue. These experiences affect your thinking and how you react to them. Your reaction to these experiences happens after you've already discussed how they affected you in your mind.

Since we identified the first self-talk type, I believe it's best to move on to the second. Can anyone guess what the second self-talk type is, if the first is "Successful Suffering Self-talk"? The second must be. Okay, maybe I didn't make it obvious enough but the second self-talk type I've noticed in my lifetime is "Self-Sabotaging Self-talk". These two types both relate to suffering, stress, pain and how we react to these types of issues. I believe we tend to talk to ourselves the most when faced with issues that affect us emotionally.

Self-Talk Type 2

Self-Sabotaging Self-Talk

Suffering doesn't always come as an external situation or problem. We are the cause of our suffering and sabotaging thoughts and internal dialogue. For example, have you ever had a time where you may have woken up late and your whole day went downhill due to how it started? Initially, everything is somewhat manageable. How you react to the initial situation determines how the day will go. Can you remember a time when being late led to forgetting an item or hurting yourself in the process? All of that may have resulted in you cutting someone off in traffic which can have potentially ended in an accident. The amount of self-sabotage inner dialogue that occurs in common situations like this is surprisingly overlooked, but this connects to the four pillars where in this case the environment and perspective have a lot to do with how the overall situation will play out.

We must learn to identify early when our actions are the cause for having something that we truly don't desire because we don't know how to correct or stop them ourselves during self-sabotage internal dialogue. All too often we continue to add to the mess we created strictly due to the narrative we have with ourselves. The mind creates pictures, and those pictures are then carried out into the words of your mind. Your thoughts are like writings on the wall of your mind. What writings are on the wall of your mind? The words we have in our minds are like little voices in our heads that no one hears.

It's the most intimate conversation you will have. Since this conversation is so close to us it has the most influence over our actions and perspective in life.

Look at how many times in a day you've gotten less than satisfactory results. Can you picture how you were thinking before you applied effort to get said results? Can you picture the type of internal dialogue you were having before you applied effort toward said results? Most of the time the destructive thoughts we have translate into the destructive world we live in. To keep both types of self-talks separate you must identify what's beneficial versus what isn't. How much time do you waste on things that can be considered waste? In the next chapter, we will discuss how to identify wasteful self-talk and how we replace it with beneficial internal dialogue.

I'm sure you heard of the proverbial head trash. In this next chapter, we will break down how that relates to our internal dialogue.

CHAPTER 4

TAKE OUT THE TRASH

Part 1: Trash or Treasure?

The term head trash has been used/ referenced in several different ways. What we tell ourselves can either be trash or treasure. When you look at the goals you do or don't set for yourself, I'm sure those goals are a part of your dreams. The dreams we have are as precious as diamonds and gold. We treat these dreams like treasures. We become frustrated, discouraged, and even confused when our lives don't line up with the goals or dreams, we have.

As I mentioned previously in this guide, every idea we see in the world was first conceived in someone's mind. The treasures of the world had to be the treasures within someone's mind first. The people who created these amazing inventions and concepts we use daily had to make a conscious effort to constantly keep beneficial dialogue in their minds for those inventions or creations to come to fruition. There's a world of difference between head treasure and trash. The trash is all the wasteful needed thoughts and self-talk we have. The worst part of head trash is that each day you can tolerate less and less. If you leave the trash in your house full for one day, it may be slightly unpleasant and stinky. If you leave your trash full for a week, the smell and pests that come with the smell will soon penetrate throughout the kitchen and the rest of the house. Now imagine if you leave the trash full for one month, your whole house will smell like the remains and waste that fills the trashcan. In the same way, physical trash can overpower the environment of your home, the trash in your head can change your environment, attitude, intentions, and actions. The head trash that comes with negative self-talk can truly determine the outcome of your entire life.

        It's somewhat delusional to think that your home will smell like lavender and roses if you don't address the waste and trash that remains in it. Our minds and lives are like our homes with excessive trash in them, they soon turn to the filth that fills within it. Most people don't even realize that the trash is starting to pile up until long after the smell and negative effects are undoubtedly evident.

    People tend to only address these matters once they become completely detrimental to their day-to-day living. Even worse some people never notice the stench of their negative self-talk and it shows in their quality of life. The most important thing to consider about self-talk is identifying the truth from lies, the fabricated from reality. Most of the trash that we have in our heads comes from the fears or emotions associated with a situation or circumstance. To truly remove head-trash you must determine if it's true or made up due to certain feelings. Before removing head-trash and replacing it with successful self-talk we must look at the root cause of head-trash.

By identifying where the head trash came from, we can properly access and determine how to remove it from our heads. The outside world plays a major role in how we speak to ourselves and the perspective we live with throughout the day. Each day we ingest several different views and opinions. Some are positive and great for our lives while some are destructive to our life and goals. I titled the daily dialogue from outside sources "Whispers of the World". The reason I call them whispers is because we are hearing, seeing, and talking in this dialogue directly and indirectly even when we're not intentionally trying to. This next section of the guide is to help determine the whispers of the world versus your whispers while determining how much these whispers create head-trash/ negative self-talk. As I mentioned we won't be able to remove and keep something away if we don't identify the root cause.

All our lives we see, hear, and feel so many different perspectives about life that aren't originally ours. As kids, we heard our parents or guardians tell us about their view on the world before we even got to establish our own. The media portrays a standard or status quo they believe we should meet. This external influence over time starts to become our inner dialogue on how we view the world to a certain extent. We learn to live our lives the way the people who influence us the most do and tend to have the same internal dialogue as those in our environment. The programming we receive is slow and gradual until you become an adult and don't even realize how much you've been influenced.

The current state of the world is due to all the experiences we've had to the present day. Imagine all the things that influenced you as a youth that you had very little control over. Do we ever think to ourselves how much of what we say, and think is truly thoughts not influenced by an external source? The external source I labeled "Whispers of the World" has been and will always be a very influential part of our lives. These whispers may be low for some or start as whispers and then turn to loud internal dialogue for others.

In this chapter, I will break down "Whispers of the World" into two parts. First, we will determine our dialogue versus the whispers of the world, then we will determine what whispers to ignore and what whispers to use as successful self-talk. Separating the type of external dialogue allows us to recognize how to use the dialogue properly to benefit our lives.

PART 2: THE WORLD'S THOUGHTS VS MY THOUGHTS

Are these my thoughts? This is a question most of us rarely, ask ourselves. How do you determine what thoughts are yours versus the ones that are influenced by external sources? If we think about it most of our thoughts aren't influenced by our emotions, perspectives, or choices. Initially, most of how we think is caused by an external condition that affects us emotionally or mentally. External situations whether negative or positive affect us internally. These external situations only become a part of our world when we allow them to assist in our ideas of what we think our lives should be.

We make up one big end game for our lives, and by doing that we consider certain things, places, and people are needed to fulfill this goal or end game. The world that surrounds us becomes our world once we determine what we want from it. Indeed, we can't control who our parents are and how and where we are born, but we can determine the world we decide to live in as we become able-bodied adults. The voice in your environment has a lot of influence on your internal dialogue. It takes a very strong trained mind to know what's truly beneficial without having to go through several years of trial and error to determine so. People rarely learn from outside teachings more than going through the pain and suffering themselves.

How do we learn to establish our thoughts and creeds without being directly related to the external world? The biggest thing we must concentrate on is how our desires, dreams, and goals relate to those around us. We tend to gravitate towards similar energies and listen to those who share the same beliefs as we do. The people we surround ourselves with reflect the self-talk we base our decisions and lives upon.

Every experience we have is an example of a life we could or couldn't have. These experiences slowly shape how we view the world, and the dialogue connected to them programs our subconscious mind on how we should speak to ourselves regarding these experiences whether personal or from outside sources. The whispers from the world aren't always negative and detrimental to our personal growth. As I previously mentioned, the idea is to align yourself with the external dialogue that reinforces your goals and dreams.

Most of our thoughts, beliefs, and ideas are based on all the external sources we receive as a youth. It takes several years to build your ideas and dialogue derived from your personal experiences, so don't feel discouraged if you still haven't found your true voice. The more you attempt to create the life you desire on the day, the more you will eventually find your voice by the process of elimination. The more you do what you aren't the closer you are to becoming who you truly desire to be. So never feel like the negative whispers of the world can't serve and benefit you. Our perspective on things that happen to us or are presented to us determines a lot about the outcome related to those events.

Below we will describe most of the external dialogue we heard growing up and the current dialogue we hear. By doing this we learn how this dialogue aligns or misaligns with our goals and dreams. The external dialogue we consistently allow to stay in our lives is a direct reflection of what we think we should or shouldn't be. Please use the blank spaces below to describe the type or direct external dialogue you heard growing up and in your present day, whether from people, media, etc.

Time:

Dialogue:

Time:

Dialogue:

Time:

Dialogue:

Time:

Dialogue:

After writing the time and dialogue down you'll be able to reference this in the future to make sure you have a clear idea of the external dialogue that influenced your self-talk. Doing this will help you become more mindful of how to properly assess the dialogue you receive from external sources in the future. We all have an idea of how we can use our environment to create the lives we want but until we learn how to remove the waste, we are blocked from utilizing all things that are directly useful in our lives. As I stated previously, everything can be a learning experience and considered useful. But there are certain circumstances where you need to evaluate if the amount of pain and trouble is worth it to understand the lesson involved or if there could have been a better way. This is why identification and self-analysis are so important to creating constant growth.

Now that we've determined how to identify our whispers versus the whispers of the world, we will establish what whispers are useful and how to use them as successful self-talk. The world will throw all types of curves, challenges, and obstacles your way, but the key is to remember that it's not about what happens to you but about how you react to those things. What happens to you, happens to everyone in some form or fashion. The issues you face someone else will face one day if they haven't already. Knowing how to use the negative things that happen to you in life to create a better situation or outcome is imperative to living a successful life.

No matter what you hear from the world you must know what's helpful to your overall goals and dreams and what may be detrimental to your goals and dreams. You need to access every word, idea and thought that comes your way and see how it may or may not align with your belief system and aspirations. If you can't tell by now, I'm a firm believer in using identification as the first step to accessing and solving any issue. This is the process that continued to assist me in overcoming addiction, substance abuse, and negative thinking.

Most people never make any progress because they don't identify a starting place. We must use our current ideologies and goals as a starting place to determine what success looks like for us. For instance, if writing this book by a certain time with a certain number of pages is what success looks like to me then I would align all the external ideas and dialogue with this goal to determine if any of it is valuable or useful to me or detrimental and a waste to me. Identification is like drawing a line in the sand to establish where you need to be within a certain goal. In the spaces below I want us to identify and establish some goals and ideas we have and with them I want us to write down some common external dialogue we hear on the day-to-day. In the next place, I want us to write if the dialogue aligns or misaligns with our goals. Lastly, I want us to determine if this dialogue needs to be kept or trashed. Before we can implement new thoughts and processes, we must first get rid of the waste that fills the space to prepare for the new and useful.

GOALS/IDEAS:

ALIGNED OR MISALIGNED:

KEEP OR TRASH:

GOALS/IDEAS:

ALIGNED OR MISALIGNED:

KEEP OR TRASH:

GOALS/IDEAS:

ALIGNED OR MISALIGNED:

KEEP OR TRASH:

GOALS/IDEAS:

ALIGNED OR MISALIGNED:

KEEP OR TRASH:

The power behind this list won't be fully recognized until you look back on it as a reference point to the goals you want to achieve, and the self-talk related to them. To get the most value out of this list, it's best to refer to it as often as possible, especially during frustration or confusion with your goals. Honestly, the goal is to use this list before you get to the point of frustration. Preventative measures go a long way when done at the right time.

Now that we know how external dialogue affects our lives and how some self-talk is a waste of our lives, I think it's time to discuss how the truth within your self-talk makes all the difference. We spend so much time trying to identify what we believe and how the things we tell ourselves play a major role in our lives that we forget to determine if the dialogue we have is even facts. The path you set for your life with the internal dialogue you have needs to be a well-established one for you to arrive at the desired destination. The best way to do that is to make sure you're living in truth and not a false reality fabricated by other factors.

We will dive deeper into the importance of separating the head trash from the truth in the coming chapter. Like they say the truth shall set you free. What's more successful than freedom?

CHAPTER 5
Truth or Trash

The most important thing about our self-talk is ensuring that the dialogue is derived from truth. With so many different voices and opinions coming from outside sources it becomes very difficult to know what truth is aligned with who you are versus what's total gibberish and a waste of time. The thoughts we have daily can be caused by so many different things that have no direct relation to our lives and beliefs. The purpose of this chapter is to determine whether the internal dialogue you have is trash made up by outside sources, emotions that led to false ideologies, or truth derived from real facts and logic.

Knowing and defining the difference between the truth you speak and the trash you tell yourself can save you a world of pain and time. Our minds can only store so much information within a certain period. How many times have you felt you were going through an overload with just dealing with too many thoughts and engagements in a day? Now picture if you had some process that allowed you to only keep the thoughts that are truly beneficial and true to your life while not holding onto or even having the ones that aren't. You would probably have way more energy and time to use your mind and internal dialogue to do more constructive tasks that are aligned with your overall purpose and goals.

The amount of time we spend conversing with ourselves on certain beliefs and ideas takes us into a downward emotional frenzy that most likely doesn't lead us to the truth or a solution. To truly determine the right thing to do you must first figure out what not to do. By doing this you place a direct opposite to what your current thinking and process may be which in turn helps empower you towards a better direction. Most people want to work on the solution without truly understanding the root cause of the issue. I believe this is counterintuitive and leads to more stress in the long run. Simply put a solution that is not centered on the root cause is essentially a temporary fix that will eventually arise again to harm you in the future.

So, if you have gotten this far into reading this guide then you understand my sentiment on the importance of identifying then addressing said thing that was identified. Below we will write a list of our most common self-talk responses to situations in our lives and write down whether it's trash or truth that we're basing our response on. There will also be a place for you to write why each self-talk response should go into a certain category.

Self-Talk Response-

Truth or Trash-

What makes this response trash or truth? -

Self-Talk Response-

Truth or Trash-

What makes this response trash or truth? -

Self-Talk Response-

Truth or Trash-

What makes this response trash or truth? -

Self-Talk Response-

Truth or Trash-

What makes this response trash or truth?

Now that we have fully embraced our current dialogue and identified what it is and isn't we can now move on to finding a way to replace our current self-talk with an internal dialogue that properly aligns with our goals and desires. It becomes very difficult to embark on new paths without having a vision or plan in place. This next chapter is designed to give you a roadmap on how to replace your current self-talk with words and phrases that better suit you. The idea is to train your mind to think of other dialogue that is the exact opposite of what you're currently stating. Essentially you will be swapping your present self-talk with the suggested self-talk in this book and any future successful self-talk words and phrases that you may come up with over time.

For that reason, this very short chapter is titled "Word & Phrase Swap". I will begin, by giving you some successful self-talk words and phrases that I currently use while showing you what words/phrases I've replaced them for. This chapter will mostly be blank lines and spaces for you to fill in for future words and phrases that you may find. When it's all said and done the goal is to completely reprogram you to instinctively speak these words and phrases without any hesitation.

CHAPTER 6
Word/Phrase Swap

1. "I Try/ I'm trying." = "Consciously Apply Effort"

2. "I Can't." = "I haven't found a way to/yet."

3. "Why is this happening to me?" = "This is happening for me."

4. "If I only had_____." = "Is there a reason or something valuable within what I currently have?"

5. "I can't wait until this is over." = "Does this time have something in it I can learn from?"

6. "Waste my time." = "Time is only wasted if a lesson isn't learned from it."

7. "I don't like_____." = "Is this true or this emotional based?"

8. "I don't know how." = "I haven't figured out or learned how to yet."

9. "This isn't enough." = "I have all I need to become all I am."

10. "This is hard." = "The difficulty will not detour or stop me."

11. "You don't understand me" = "I respect your perspective about me."

12._____

_____

_____

_____

_____

_____

_____

This list will be a great reference for you when you are having a hard time finding the right words to help change your perspective. I strongly advise you to get used to saying these words and phrases while using your current dialogue, so that it feels like a seamless transition to your newfound self-talk dialogue. If anything, I suggest you use your current dialogue even more, so you become even more aware and familiar with what you are saying on the daily. By doing this you will see a drastic change in the difference between what you were saying and your newly adopted dialogue.

CHAPTER 7
Success Starts with Speech
(Conclusion)

If you could explain what success means to you in one sentence what would say? Is there anything you think you will have to include to solidify your statement? What would you base your viewpoint on? Success looks different to everyone in my opinion. There is a common ground we all stand on when it comes to how we view success and what we believe it is. You know this is true by how some people are commonly liked and praised compared to others. I've always wondered what made someone aspire to be like someone else. Is it the fact there is something special each person sees in that person? Is it because other people favor this person as well? It may be a mix of both for some, but for me, I've always looked up to those who exemplified certain characteristics that I wanted to see in myself.

All these people shared similar characteristics amongst each other. They all were successful in areas that I valued for myself and verbalized their belief for their goals externally to the world. They also shared how their internal dialogue made all the difference. We essentially look at the world as an example of things we do or don't want for ourselves, and we follow suit. The things that make us similar are the exact things that make us different because we all have desires, goals, and things we want out of our lives. The pursuit and acquisition of our goals is what makes us similar. We all have this fire that lives within us whether it's a blazing desire or a small flame that dwindles, it's still stored within every human being. There are two things in my opinion that makes everyone different. The first is the specific thing that you desire to acquire and the second is what you do with this small or large fire that burns within you.

The people who have answers to both of those questions and execute those answers are the ones that inspired me the most. That is the most common trait among all the people we admire in this world. They identified and determined what success meant to them and executed with that in mind. Success starts within your mind first and the everyday dialogue you have with yourself. All lives fall in between the daily affirmations of failure and confusion or the daily affirmations of abundance and focus. These are the building blocks of the world you create outside of you. The statement as above so below is equally stated, as within, so without. The world we decide to create outside of ourselves will only reflect what lies within us. These statements are so true because you see this in the everyday lives of the people around you. If you don't believe me then I challenge, you to try this experiment and take note of the results internally.

The challenge is, I want you to think of two people you are close with. This can be a close friend, co-worker, or family member, it doesn't matter. You just need to know a little about how they think and have been in their home or car a handful of times. Try to also think of two people who are different in the aspect of how they plan and organize their conversations and lives. Think of two people if you can that are somewhat opposites. One person may be more of a communicator, planner and organized and the other may be a not-so-good communicator, planner, and more on the messy side. Now ask yourself once you get these two different people in your mind. Does the person who is a better planner, clear communicator, and organized have a more peaceful presence and cleaner environment, whether that be home or car? Now ask yourself the same question for the other person. Is the person who doesn't communicate as well and not as organized, has a messier environment. The answer will most likely be yes. They have done studies that people who have more peaceful thoughts and have better internal dialogue tend to have cleaner and more organized environments.

    This by no means makes one person better than the other. I'm sure each person has different strengths and weaknesses. We are all constant works in progress, but I say this to say that this just proves the statement as within, so without. The life we desire to have, live and love begins within and how we program our minds with those small little internal whispers we tell ourselves every day. The conversations that no one hears are the ones that affect our lives the most. Before you start having conversations with the world on how to obtain all you wish for, make sure your relationship with yourself and self-talk is as good as it can be. This conversation outweighs any conversation you will have with anyone else.

Now to answer my question of *what success means to you in one sentence*, in my opinion, success is the desired result of any action. There will be times when your mind wants to go to places that don't serve you but remember the path to your success starts with the speech you have within. I hope that this guide can successfully assist you on your journey to acquire all you desire. The world you wish to live in has already begun building. Each word you say on a daily either lays a brick in the path to your destruction or the path to your dreams and desires. Always remember success starts with your speech. With all the love and faith stay well and be conscious. Your ally and friend Julian.

www.ingramcontent.com/pod-product-compliance
Lightning Source LLC
Chambersburg PA
CBHW052205070526
44585CB00017B/2079